Pearls of Wisdom

Compiled and Illustrated by
Constanze von Kitzing

Bahá'í
PUBLISHING

Bahá'í Publishing
401 Greenleaf Avenue, Wilmette, Illinois 60091
Copyright © 2014 by the
National Spiritual Assembly of the
Bahá'ís of the United States

17 16 15 14   4   3   2   1

Library of Congress Cataloging-in-Publication Data
Pearls of wisdom / compiled and Illustrated by Constanze von Kitzing.
       pages cm
  Includes bibliographical references.
  ISBN 978-1-61851-069-3 (alk. paper)
  1. Bahai Faith—Juvenile literature. I. Von Kitzing, Constanze, editor of compilation.
  BP366.P43 2014
  297.9'3432—dc23

                      2013045860

Book design by Patrick Falso
Illustrations by Constanze von Kitzing

Introduction

Do you ever think about God, and wonder Who or what He is? Do you ever wonder about your soul? Do you think about love and friendship and service to others? What do these words mean to you? *Pearls of Wisdom* is a book designed to make you think about these words and to reflect on what they might mean. The words in this book all come from the Central Figures of the Bahá'í Faith. The Bahá'í Faith is a religion for all the people of the world. Bahá'ís believe that there is just one God, that all of the major religions of the world come from that same God, and that all people belong to one human family. It is hoped that parents and children will enjoy this book together and that it will lead to many interesting conversations about important topics.

God

The beginning of all things is the knowledge of God.[1]

The One true God may be compared unto the sun and the believer unto a mirror. No sooner is the mirror placed before the sun than it reflects its light.[2]

The Soul

Behold how the light of the sun illuminates the world of matter: even so doth the Divine Light shed its rays in the kingdom of the soul. The soul it is which makes the human creature a celestial entity![3]

Turn thy sight unto thyself, that thou mayest find Me standing within thee, mighty, powerful and self-subsisting.[4]

Man

O SON OF BEING!
Thou art My lamp and My light is in thee. Get thou from it thy radiance and seek none other than Me. For I have created thee rich and have bountifully shed My favor upon thee.[5]

O SON OF SPIRIT!
My first counsel is this: Possess a pure, kindly and radiant heart, that thine may be a sovereignty ancient, imperishable and everlasting.[6]

Prayer

Immerse yourselves in the ocean of My words, that ye may unravel its secrets, and discover all the pearls of wisdom that lie hid in its depths.[7]

The reason why privacy hath been enjoined in moments of devotion is this, that thou mayest give thy best attention to the remembrance of God, that thy heart may at all times be animated with His Spirit, and not be shut out as by a veil from thy Best Beloved.[8]

The Image of God

O SON OF MAN!
Veiled in My immemorial being and in the ancient eternity of My essence, I knew My love for thee; therefore I created thee, have engraved on thee Mine image and revealed to thee My beauty.[9]

Regard man as a mine rich in gems of inestimable value. Education can, alone, cause it to reveal its treasures, and enable mankind to benefit therefrom.[10]

Perfection

Let each morn be better than its eve and each morrow richer than its yesterday. Man's merit lieth in service and virtue and not in the pageantry of wealth and riches. Take heed that your words be purged from idle fancies and worldly desires and your deeds be cleansed from craftiness and suspicion.[11]

Therefore strive that your actions day by day may be beautiful prayers. Turn towards God, and seek always to do that which is right and noble.[12]

Unity

If any differences arise amongst you, behold Me standing before your face, and overlook the faults of one another for My name's sake and as a token of your love for My manifest and resplendent Cause.[13]

Ye are the fruits of one tree, and the leaves of one branch. Deal ye one with another with the utmost love and harmony, with friendliness and fellowship.[14]

Friendship

One must see in every human being only that which is worthy of praise. When this is done, one can be a friend to the whole human race. If, however, we look at people from the standpoint of their faults, then being a friend to them is a formidable task.[15]

A kindly tongue is the lodestone of the hearts of men. It is the bread of the spirit, it clotheth the words with meaning, it is the fountain of the light of wisdom and understanding.[16]

Love

The best way to thank God is to love one another.[17]

So far as ye are able, ignite a candle of love in every meeting, and with tenderness rejoice and cheer ye every heart. Care for the stranger as for one of your own; show to alien souls the same loving kindness ye bestow upon your faithful friends.[18]

Peace

Love is the objective point of peace, and peace is an outcome of love.[19]

Sow not, O people, the seeds of dissension amongst men, and contend not with your neighbor. Be patient under all conditions, and place your whole trust and confidence in God.[20]

Service

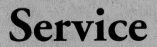

This is the Day in which God's most excellent favors have been poured out upon men, the Day in which His most mighty grace hath been infused into all created things.[21]

That one indeed is a man who, today, dedicateth himself to the service of the entire human race.[22]

The Love of God

For every one of you his paramount duty is to choose for himself that on which no other may infringe and none usurp from him. Such a thing—and to this the Almighty is My witness—is the love of God, could ye but perceive it.[23]

All things proceed from God and unto Him they return.
He is the source of all things and in Him all things are ended.[24]

References

1. Bahá'u'lláh, *Gleanings from the Writings of Bahá'u'lláh*, no. 2.1.
2. The Báb, *Selections from the Writings of the Báb*, no. 3:31:1.
3. 'Abdu'l-Bahá, *Paris Talks*, no. 28.6.
4. Bahá'u'lláh, The Hidden Words, Arabic, no. 13.
5. Ibid., no. 11.
6. Ibid., no. 1.
7. Bahá'u'lláh, *Gleanings from the Writings of Bahá'u'lláh*, no. 70.2.
8. The Báb, *Selections from the Writings of the Báb*, no. 3:21:1.
9. Bahá'u'lláh, The Hidden Words, Arabic, no. 3.
10. Bahá'u'lláh, *Gleanings from the Writings of Bahá'u'lláh*, no. 122.1.
11. Bahá'u'lláh, *Tablets of Bahá'u'lláh*, p. 138.
12. 'Abdu'l-Bahá, *Paris Talks*, no. 26.7.
13. Bahá'u'lláh, *Gleanings from the Writings of Bahá'u'lláh*, no. 146.1.
14. Bahá'u'lláh, Epistle to the Son of the Wolf, p. 14.
15. 'Abdu'l-Bahá, *Selections from the Writings of 'Abdu'l-Bahá*, no. 144.2.
16. Bahá'u'lláh, *Gleanings from the Writings of Bahá'u'lláh*, no. 132.5.
17. 'Abdu'l-Bahá, *The Promulgation of Universal Peace*, p. 661.
18. 'Abdu'l-Bahá, *Selections from the Writings of 'Abdu'l-Bahá*, no. 16.5.
19. 'Abdu'l-Bahá, *The Promulgation of Universal Peace*, p. 234.
20. Bahá'u'lláh, *Gleanings from the Writings of Bahá'u'lláh*, no. 136.4.
21. Ibid., no. 4.1.
22. Ibid. no. 117.1.
23. Ibid., no. 123.3.
24. Bahá'u'lláh, The Kitáb-i-Aqdas, ¶144.

Bibliography

Works of Bahá'u'lláh

Epistle to the Son of the Wolf. Translated by Shoghi Effendi. 1st ps ed. Wilmette, IL: Bahá'í Publishing Trust, 1988.

Gleanings from the Writings of Bahá'u'lláh. Translated by Shoghi Effendi. Wilmette, IL: Bahá'í Publishing, 2005.

The Hidden Words. Translated by Shoghi Effendi. Wilmette, IL: Bahá'í Publishing, 2002.

The Kitáb-i-Aqdas: The Most Holy Book. 1st ps ed. Wilmette, IL: Bahá'í Publishing Trust, 1993.

Tablets of Bahá'u'lláh revealed after the Kitáb-i-Aqdas. Compiled by the Research Department of the Universal House of Justice. Translated by Habib Taherzadeh et al. Wilmette, IL: Bahá'í Publishing Trust, 1988.

Works of the Báb

Selections from the Writings of the Báb. Compiled by the Research Department of the Universal House of Justice. Translated by Habib Taherzadeh et al. Wilmette, IL: Bahá'í Publishing Trust, 2006.

Works of 'Abdu'l-Bahá

Paris Talks: Addresses Given By 'Abdu'l-Bahá in Paris in 1911. Wilmette, IL: Bahá'í Publishing, 2011.

Promulgation of Universal Peace: Talks Delivered by 'Abdu'l-Bahá during His Visit to the United States and Canada in 1912. Compiled by Howard MacNutt. Wilmette, IL: Bahá'í Publishing, 2012.

Selections from the Writings of 'Abdu'l-Bahá. Compiled by the Research Department of the Universal House of Justice. Translated by a Committee at the Bahá'í World Center and Marzieh Gail. Wilmette, IL: Bahá'í Publishing, 2010.